Someone Is Speaking: Are You Listening?

Second Edition

B.L. Allen

I0152932

Someone Is Speaking:
Are You Listening?
Second Edition

Copyright © 2012
Betty Allen
B.L. Allen's Ministries

*Unless otherwise indicated, all Scripture quotations are from
the King James Version of the Bible.*

LCCN: 2011961976
ISBN: 978-0-9832682-1-5
First printing: November 2011
Second printing: May 2012
For information, contact:
B.L. Allen's Ministries
P.O. Box 37692
Shreveport, LA 71133
(318) 617-8482
Please visit http://blallenministries.webs.com
Email address: ballenboop2@yahoo.com
Printed in the USA by
Morris Publishing®

3212 Hwy. 30E • Kearney, NE 68847
800-650-7888 www.morrispublishing.com

Dedication

I dedicate this book to my parents, who instilled in me the art of being persistent and taught me how to be consistent in studying the word of God.

•

It was my mother who taught me how to read the Bible persistently, and it was my father who taught me how to be a consistent church member. As an inspirational speaker and writer, I pray I will have a positive impact on other individuals' lives as my parents had on mine.

Contents

Acknowledgments
Introduction

Response

About the Author

Acknowledgments

Father in the Name of Jesus, O God, thou hast taught me from my youth and hitherto have I declared thy wondrous works. Now also when I am old and grey headed, O God, forsake me not; until I have shewed thy strength unto this generation, and thy power to everyone that is to come. Psalm 71:17-18

I first want to thank God for giving me the ability to write this book to be an inspiration to others.

I fear I will leave out a name, so I won't list every single person who helped make this book possible. But please know that I love you, and I appreciate you.

I do want to publicly thank one particular person, who helped stir in me a desire to share the words in this book. To the late Pastor J.B. Simmons, I want to say thank you, because you told me that God was speaking and this is what he said: "Ye shall walk in all the ways which the Lord your God hath commanded you, that ye may live, and that it may be well with you, and that ye may prolong your days in the land ye shall possess." Deuteronomy 5:33

I thank my family for your continued support, and I thank my friends for encouraging me.

Introduction

I titled this book, *Someone Is Speaking: Are You Listening?* because I wanted to focus on the voice behind the scriptures, the voice of God. Just think of it as having a little talk with Jesus. Think of God as your life coach. When you listen to him, you in turn will do good things, feel good, and have joy. And oh, yes, by the way, there will be some pain.

Just like with exercise, you will have a few aches and pains in order to get the beautiful results. With exercise, you want to have that beautiful body. With life, you want to have that beautiful day-to-day existence.

Are you ready to make and keep your new life's career resolutions just by listening when God speaks and doing what you hear him say? You can do this by finding the Biblical scriptures that can help you meet your goals.

Three key steps to making resolutions stick:
1. Establishing clear objectives
2. Identifying specific steps to pursue your goals
3. Being consistent

I wrote this book especially for students and young people. This book aims to help you understand God's Word and see how it applies to your life today. Adults will enjoy the book too.

When it comes to God, he uses ministers as his life coaches, the Holy Spirit as a life teacher, and the Bible as a life manual. "And I will give you **pastors** according to mine heart, which shall feed you with knowledge and understanding," God says in Jeremiah 3:15.

Ministers are supposed to guide you with the Word of God, which is the life plan that God has given. They are also supposed to help you find support for what they are teaching in the Bible, to guide you along life's journey.

Like guidance counselors do at school to help you select a college to attend, what courses to take, and your career path, as well as tell you to attend classes three times a week, ministers provide insight and direction.

God asks us to write out a plan for our lives in Habakkuk 2:2 "And the Lord answered me, and said, write the vision, and make it plain upon tables, that he may run that readeth it."

Follow God's plan, and you will see a positive change in your life. So start your new life today. Someone is speaking, so please listen.

Chapter One

Know Who You Are in Christ Jesus

Haven't started your life plan yet? Don't worry. It's not too late. God gives us brand new mercy every day when he wakes us up.

Some of you might even say, "I didn't even know that there was a life plan just for my life."

Well, you are not alone. Many individuals do not know this.

Just for a few minutes think back to when you were in high school and had an appointment to meet with the guidance counselor. Maybe the purpose was to discuss your options following graduation: Would you attend college? If so, which one? Would you go into the military? Would you go directly into the workforce?

In the case here, God will be the guidance counselor. Let us have a dialogue with him. In the following conversation, your Someone is Speaking Moment is where God talks to you through his word. The Are You Listening Moment is the time for you to truly reflect on what God said and see how it applies to your life.

Someone Is Speaking Moment: God speaks in Jeremiah 29:11, "For I know the thoughts that I think toward you, saith the LORD, thoughts of peace, and not of evil, to give you an expected end."

Are You Listening Moment: Now did you hear what God said? He said that his thoughts about you and your life are thoughts of peace and not of evil, to give you a bright future. God *wants* good things for you! He desires that you have a life of joy and peace, filled with love. Is that the life you have now? If not, what can you do to get it? Do you need to make adjustments in your actions, attitude, and beliefs to help you get the kind of life God has for you?

Someone Is Speaking Moment: God speaks in 3 John 1:2, "Beloved, I wish above all things that thou mayest prosper and be in health, even as thy soul prospereth."

Are You Listening Moment: God calls you "beloved" (individuals who have accepted him as their Lord and Savior). He says that he wishes that you may prosper and be in health. This further supports the previous Someone is Speaking Moment, where God told us he wants peace for us. Here, he tells us he wants us to prosper! Many times, we think our lives should be hard and filled with sacrifice and tough times. And while tough times and sacrifice both come with a life lived in God's word, this scripture lets us know that our lives don't have to be about constant struggle and sacrifice. If you are living a life that seems to be filled with more hard times than good times and more doing without than living with abundance, pray and ask God to show you how to change your reality.

Refuse to continue to live a life of struggle, hardship, and pain. Invite God into your life and let him shower you with his blessings.

God wants you to have the best that life has to offer and he wants you in good health. God does not want you sick, weak, frail, and barely making it.

Just like many schools start career training classes and programs in January and August, God lets us start a new life every minute of every twenty-four hours that he gives us air to breathe. We can make a change at any time, if only we resolve in our hearts to do so. It is never too late to start a new life program with God.

Someone Is Speaking Moment: God says in Philippians 1:6, "Being confident of this very thing, that he which hath begun a good work in you will perform it until the day of Jesus Christ."

Are You Listening Moment: God said that what he has begun in you, he will make sure that you will finish it in your lifetime. It will all be good with you. Are you letting God start a new work in you? If so, how has your life changed since that new work began? If not, why not?

Someone Is Speaking Moment: God says in 2 Corinthians 5:17, "Therefore if any man be in Christ, he is a new creature: old things are passed away; behold all things are become New."

Are You Listening Moment: God said anyone who comes to him and tells him that he/she accepts him as their Lord and savior is a new person. All the old things are gone for good and he/she is a new person with a new beginning.

Someone Is Speaking Moment: God is speaking in Philippians 4:19, "But my God shall supply all your need according to his riches in glory by Christ Jesus."

Are You Listening Moment: God is telling you that now you have accepted him, he will take care of all your needs, no matter what they are. This is an amazing assurance! No longer are you alone, feeling as if it is you against the world. God has your back. He is on your side. He will take care of you. If you've ever been in a tough situation and you were not sure how you could possibly come out of it, but somehow you did, then that was God. God makes the impossible happen.

Someone Is Speaking Moment: God is speaking in 1 Timothy 2:3- 4. "For this is good and acceptable in the sight of God our savior; who will have all men to be saved, and to come unto the knowledge of the truth."

Are you Listening Moment: Did you hear God say anyone can have all of his mercy, grace, love, and forgiveness? How does that make you feel? If you are in a position right now where you feel nobody loves, cares about, or understands you, then know that God does. He welcomes you with open arms.

Someone Is Speaking Moment: "Jesus answered and said unto him (Nicodemus), Verily, verily, I say unto thee, Except a man be born again, he cannot see the Kingdom of God.

"Nicodemus saith unto him, how can man be born when he is old? Can he enter the second time into his mother's womb, and be born?

"Jesus answered, Verily, verily, I say unto thee, Except a man be born of water and of the Spirit, he cannot enter into the Kingdom of God.

"That which is born of the flesh is flesh; and that which is born of the Spirit is spirit. Marvel not that I said unto thee, Ye must be born again." John 3:3-7

Well, who qualifies for this new birth? You do. We all do. Because, sometimes you wish that you could start your life over. It's true. Jesus is speaking to you here to let you know that you can start over. So how about it? Are you ready to start over?

Someone Is Speaking Moment: God speaks in Romans 3:10 "As it is written, there is none righteous, no, not one."

Are You Listening Moment: Did you hear what God said, that everyone is qualified, every race is acceptable to qualify, because no one individual is so good, so right, so rich, so poor, so sick, so weak, so frail; there are none righteous. Everyone qualifies for the new birth.

Someone Is Speaking Moment: God speaks in Romans 3:23, "For all have sinned, and come short of the glory of God."

Are You Listening Moment: All individuals have sinned. That means you don't have to feel that you are the worst person there is. Nor do you have to feel as if you are somehow a black sheep. In God's eyes, we have all done wrong. And that means no one is any better than anyone else. So stop walking around feeling as if you can never measure up to those around you. You don't have to measure up to them. All you have to do is seek God, ask his forgiveness, and ask him to change your heart. You don't have to compete with those around you. Just be a better person today than you were yesterday.

Someone Is Speaking Moment: God speaks in Romans 5:8, "But God commanded his love toward us, in that, while we were yet sinners, Christ died for us."

Are You Listening Moment: Did you hear God say that He has taken care of all of our sin? Because he loves us. Jesus absolutely adores you. He loves you so much that he was willing to hang on a cross for you. For you and me he hung on a cross. What does that say to you?

Someone Is Speaking Moment: God speaks in Romans 6:23, "For the wages of sin is death, but the gift of God is eternal life through Jesus Christ our Lord."

Are You Listening Moment: Did you hear God say that when you choose him, Jesus Christ, you will receive eternal life? When you choose to sin, it will bring death. Will you choose life?

Someone Is Speaking Moment: God speaks in Romans 10:9-13 "That if thou shalt confess with thy mouth the Lord Jesus and shalt believe in thine heart that God hath raised him from the dead, thou shalt be saved. For with the heart man believeth unto righteousness; and with the mouth confession is made unto salvation. For the scripture saith, whosoever believeth on him shall not be ashamed. For there is no difference between the Jew and the Greek: for the same Lord over all is rich unto all that call upon him. For whosoever shall call upon the name of the Lord shall be saved."

Are You Listening Moment: God said come unto him and accept him by confessing with your mouth that he is your Lord and Savior.

Someone Is Speaking Moment: God spoke in Isaiah 54:17B, "No weapon that is formed against thee shall prosper; and every tongue that shall rise against thee in judgment thou shalt condemn. *This is the heritage of the servants of the LORD, and their righteousness is of me, saith the LORD."*

Are You Listening Moment: Did you hear God say that your righteousness is of me? That means the only thing you have to do is to confess with your mouth that he is your Lord and Savior and believe that he died on the cross for you. Then you will know who you are in Christ Jesus.

Someone Is Speaking Moment: God is speaking in Jeremiah 1:5, "Before I formed thee in the belly I knew thee; and before thou camest forth out of the womb I sanctified thee, and I ordained thee a prophet unto the nations."

Are You Listening Moment: God said that before you were born, before he placed you in your mother's womb, that he decided the color of your pigmentation, your culture, your nationality, the length of your hair, the color of your eyes, the width of your hips, your talents, and your height.

Also God sanctified you and ordained your life plan. All of this took place before he placed you in your mother's womb, before you were born. You are here intentionally. You were no accident and your life has tremendous meaning. God brought you here for a reason. Now that you know this, how will that affect the decisions you make?

Someone Is Speaking Moment: God is speaking in Psalm 23:1, "The LORD is my shepherd; I shall not want."

Are You Listening Moment: Here God lets us know through David that he is our protector and provider. There is not a single need you have that God cannot meet. Think about the challenges that are facing you right now. If you've been feeling that you don't know how you will face them, then place them all in God's hands now. Do this by praying to him and asking him to show you how to handle each one. Ask him to provide the answer, and he will, just as his word says.

Someone Is Speaking Moment: God speaks in Proverbs 4:20-22 "My son, (daughters) attend to my words; incline thine ear unto my sayings.²¹Let them not depart from thine eyes; keep them in the midst of thine heart.²²For they are life unto those that find them, and health to all their flesh."

Are You Listening Moment: This is really cool, but what happens when I find myself in trouble with my classes or failing in life? What should I do then?

Someone Is Speaking Moment: God is speaking in Psalm 107:19-20, "Then they cry unto the LORD in their trouble, and he saveth them out of their distresses. ²⁰He sent his word, and healed them, and delivered them from their destructions."

Someone Is Speaking Moment: God speaks in Luke 12:7, "But even the very hairs of your head are all numbered. Fear not therefore: ye are of more value than many sparrows."

   Are You Listening Moment: God is telling you that he is so concerned about you that he hears your cry and saves you from your distresses. He loves you so much that he even pays attention to everything about you. In fact, he knows the number of hairs that you have on your head, the ones that have permanent color, semi-permanent color and even the ones that are highlighted with Dark-N-Lovely, Nice and Easy, and Revlon Colorsilk.

He knows more about you than you know about yourself. How does it make you feel to realize that God knows and loves you that much? As you go about your day today, think about this and see if it affects how you see your life.

Someone Is Speaking Moment: God is speaking in Isaiah 55:11-12[11] "So shall my word be that goeth forth out of my mouth: it shall not return unto me void, but it shall accomplish that which I please, and it shall prosper in the thing whereto I sent it."

Are You Listening Moment: You may be surprised when you read that salvation comes by grace through faith and will contrast the difference between Christianity and other religions of the world. It's very imperative to understand what happens when you receive Jesus as your savior. It's the answer to keeping the word that was sown in your heart from being stolen by Satan. God gives us solid scriptural foundation that will help you understand. Remember he is your guidance counselor and he has life coaches in place for you to talk with.

As you read through these Are You Listening Moments, you might start to think back to all the times you've said "No" to God. You might even think you are a bad person. Just realize that saying "No" to God is a symptom of "the disease to please the world." "Saying "No" when you need to say "Yes" causes burnout or death. You do yourself and the person making the request a disservice by saying "No" all of the time, to eternal life. Here's how to do the right thing for yourself and others: Don't feel guilty. Just take these scriptures from the Bible on protocol and communication – and a clue from your guidance counselor, creator, and savior – and say "Yes."

Someone Is Speaking Moment: God is speaking in Deuteronomy 30:19, "I call heaven and earth to record this day against you that I have set before you life and death, blessing and cursing: therefore **choose life**, that both thou and thy seed may live."

Are You Listening Moment: Will I learn through scripture that true salvation includes, but is not limited to, the forgiveness of our sins? It's the forgiveness of sins that makes close fellowship with the Lord possible, but much more was provided, more than you may have ever imagined.

Someone Is Speaking Moment: God is speaking in 1 Corinthians 2:9, "But as it is written, Eye hath not seen, nor ear heard, neither have entered into the heart of man, the things which God hath prepared for them that love him."

Are You Listening Moment: This is such an amazing scripture! It lets me know that God has so many wonderful things in store for us that we can't even imagine. Now, isn't that exciting? How does that make you feel?

Someone Is Speaking Moment: God speaks again in Isaiah 64:4, "For since the beginning of the world men have not heard, nor perceived by the ear, neither hath the eye seen, O God, beside thee, what he hath prepared for him that waiteth for him."

Are You Listening Moment: Have you realized just how cool it is to say "Yes," to Jesus? You can talk with him at any time of the day or night about your problems. And you can talk with him when everything is going well, too.

Therefore, you have a new life and a new life coach when you say "Yes" to Jesus, because he is in you talking to you all the time about everything.

I like what I am hearing!!!
I like what I am hearing!!!
I like what I am hearing!!!

Someone Is Speaking

Chapter Two

Know Your Benefits in Christ Jesus

The guidance counselor tells you what you will get out of going to college or joining the military, attending a trade school, or not attending school at all. The positive things are called benefits. Remember if you let God be your guidance counselor and let the ministers he has called be your life coach, you will receive benefits in his life plan also.

You might now be thinking, "What are some of the benefits of choosing to listen to God?"

Are they like the benefits on a job, such as 40lK, annual leave, sick leave, health insurance, vision insurance, unemployment insurance, FLMA, maternity leave, social security, Medicaid, Medicare, and retirement?

Well, God tells you here. Check it out.

Someone Is Speaking Moment: God is speaking about benefits in Psalm 1:1-3 [1] "Blessed is the man that walketh not in the counsel of the ungodly, nor standeth in the way of sinners, nor sitteth in the seat of the scornful. [2]But his delight is in the law of the LORD; and in his law doth he meditate day and night. [3]And he shall be like a tree planted by the rivers of water, that bringeth forth his fruit in his season; his leaf also shall not wither; and whatsoever he doeth shall prosper."

Are You Listening Moment: Did you hear God telling you about your Benefits? He said if you walk not in the counsel of people who give you wrong advice then you are blessed. He went on to say if you do not stop people from coming to Christ, you are blessed, and if you do not sit back using criticism against others then you are blessed.

Someone Is Speaking Moment: God is speaking. He is telling you about your health plan, and your insurance plan. And let me tell you, that insurance plan is better than BlueCross/Blue Shield. In Psalm 103: 1-22, he says, "[1]Bless the LORD, O my soul: and all that is within me, bless his holy name.[2]Bless the LORD, O my soul, and forget not all **his benefits:**[3]Who forgiveth all thine iniquities; who healeth all thy diseases;[4]Who redeemeth thy life from destruction; who crowneth thee with loving kindness and tender mercies;[5]Who satisfieth thy mouth with good things; so that thy youth is renewed like the eagle's.[6]The LORD executeth righteousness and judgment for all that are oppressed.[7]He made known his ways unto Moses, his acts unto the children of Israel.[8]The LORD is merciful and gracious, slow to anger, and plenteous in mercy.[9]He will not always chide: neither will he keep his anger forever.[10]He hath not dealt with us after our sins; nor rewarded us according to our iniquities.[11]For as the heaven is high above the earth, so great is his mercy toward them that fear him.[12]As far as the east is from the west, so far hath he removed our transgressions from us.[13]Like as a father pitieth his children, so the LORD pitieth them that fear him.[14]For he knoweth our frame; he remembereth that we are dust.[15]As for man, his days are as grass: as a flower of the field, so he flourisheth.[16]For the wind passeth over it, and it is gone; and the place thereof shall know it no more.[17]But the mercy of the LORD is from everlasting to everlasting upon them that fear him, and his righteousness unto children's children;[18]To such as keep his covenant, and to those that remember his commandments to do them.[19]The LORD hath prepared his throne in the heavens; and his kingdom ruleth over all.[20]Bless the LORD, ye his angels, that excel in strength, that do his commandments, hearkening unto the voice of his word.[21]Bless ye the LORD, all ye his hosts; ye ministers of his, that do his pleasure.[22]Bless the LORD, all his works in all places of his dominion: bless the LORD, O my soul."

So many Benefits, I think I lost count.

That is o.k. I will list them for you.

God spoke of 20 benefits in the health plan. I will number each one of them for you here:

1. God forgiveth all (your) thine <u>iniquities.</u>
2. God healeth all (your) thy <u>diseases</u> (yes, all diseases that includes preexisting diseases, cancer, AIDS, etc.).
3. God redeemeth (your) thy <u>life from destruction.</u>
4. God crowneth (you) thee <u>with loving kindness.</u>
5. God crowneth (you) thee <u>with tender mercies.</u>
6. God satisfieth (your) thy <u>mouth with good things so</u> (your) thy <u>youth is renewed like the eagle's.</u>
7. God executeth righteousness and judgment for (you) all <u>that are oppressed.</u>
8. God will make known his ways unto (you) Moses<u>, his acts unto</u> (you) the children.
9. God is merciful and gracious, slow to anger, and plenteous in mercy toward (you).
10. God will not always chide (express disapproval), neither will he keep his anger forever at (you).
11. God hath not dealt with (you) us <u>after our sins;</u> nor rewarded us according to our iniquities.
12. God hath removed (your) our <u>transgressions from</u> (you) us, <u>as far as the heaven is high above the earth and as far as the east is from the west.</u> He will give you mercy in place of your transgressions.
13. God pitieth (you) them <u>that fear him.</u>

14. God knows (your) our <u>frame;</u> he remembereth that (you) we <u>are dust</u>. (We all are made out of dust)

15. God knows (you) man, his <u>days are as grass;</u> as a flower of the field, so he flourisheth, for the wind passeth over it, and is gone, and the place thereof shall know it no more. He knows the number of days that (you) have on this earth. But the mercy of the Lord is from everlasting to everlasting upon them that fear him, and his righteousness unto children's children; to such as keep his covenant, and to those that remember his commandments to do them. Psalm 103:17

16. God hath prepared His throne in the heavens; and His kingdom ruleth over all.

17. God hath angels that excel in strength, that do His commandments, hearkening unto the voice of His word <u>for you.</u>

18. God hath the heavenly hosts, his ministers that do his pleasure <u>that work for you.</u>

19. God hath everything in place <u>to bless you;</u> all his works in all places of his dominion.

20. God has this full health plan <u>just for you.</u>

Are You Listening Moment: God outlines so many blessings here that you probably lost count! His benefits are better than any other plan you can think of — and his benefits are guaranteed!

Someone Is Speaking Moment: God uses Paul to talk about other benefits in Ephesians 1:1-16:

¹Paul, an apostle of Jesus Christ by the will of God, to the saints which are at Ephesus, and to the faithful in Christ Jesus:

²Grace be to you, and peace, from God our Father, and from the Lord Jesus Christ.

³Blessed be the God and Father of our Lord Jesus Christ, who hath <u>blessed us with all spiritual blessings in heavenly places in Christ:</u>

⁴According as <u>he hath chosen us</u> in him before the foundation of the world, that we should be holy and without blame before him in love:

⁵Having <u>predestinated us unto the adoption of children by Jesus Christ to himself,</u> according to the good pleasure of his will,

⁶To the praise of the glory of his grace, wherein <u>he hath made us accepted in the beloved.</u>

⁷In whom <u>we have redemption through his blood</u>, the forgiveness of sins, according to the riches of his grace;

[8]Wherein <u>he hath abounded toward us in all wisdom</u> and prudence;

[9]Having <u>made known unto us the mystery of his will,</u> according to his good pleasure which he hath purposed in himself:

[10]That in the dispensation of the fulness of times he might gather together in one all things in Christ, both which are in heaven, and which are on earth; even in him:

[11]In whom also <u>we have obtained an inheritance,</u> being predestinated according to the purpose of him who worketh all things after the counsel of his own will:

[12]That we should be to the praise of his glory, who first trusted in Christ.

[13]In whom ye also trusted, after that ye heard the word of truth, the gospel of your salvation: in whom also after that ye believed, ye were sealed with that Holy Spirit of promise,

[14]Which is the earnest of <u>our inheritance until the redemption</u> of the purchased possession, unto the praise of his glory.

[15]Wherefore I also, after I heard of your faith in the Lord Jesus, and love unto all the saints,

[16]Cease not to give thanks for you, making mention of you in my prayers;

Are You Listening Moment: This benefit plan Paul spoke about is full of even more blessings just for us. It is great. It is so rich. There were sixteen benefits in this plan alone.

Someone Is Speaking Moment: God is telling you how your blessing plan works in Psalm 91: 1-16:

[1]He that dwelleth in the secret place of the most High shall abide under the shadow of the Almighty.[2]I will say of the LORD, He is my refuge and my fortress: my God; in him will I trust. [3]Surely he shall deliver thee from the snare of the fowler, and from the noisome pestilence. [4]He shall cover thee with his feathers, and under his wings shalt thou trust: his truth shall be thy shield and buckler. [5]Thou shalt not be afraid for the terror by night; nor for the arrow that flieth by day; [6]Nor for the pestilence that walketh in darkness; nor for the destruction that wasteth at noonday. [7]A thousand shall fall at thy side, and ten thousand at thy right hand; but it shall not come nigh thee. [8]Only with thine eyes shalt thou behold and see the reward of the wicked. [9]Because thou hast made the LORD, which is my refuge, even the most High, thy habitation; [10]There shall no evil befall thee, neither shall any plague come nigh thy dwelling. [11]For he shall give his angels charge over thee, to keep thee in all thy ways. [12]They shall bear thee up in their hands, lest thou dash thy foot against a stone. [13]Thou shalt tread upon the lion and adder: the young lion and the dragon shalt thou trample under feet.[14]Because he hath set his love upon me, therefore will I deliver him: I will set him on high, because he hath known my name. [15]He shall call upon me, and I will answer him: I will be with him in trouble; I will deliver him, and honour him. [16]With long life will I satisfy him, and shew him my salvation.

Are You Listening Moment: By now, you might just be wondering, "When do I get paid?" You can start collecting your benefits now, if you decide to sign on to God's plan.

Someone Is Speaking Moment: God is speaking in Malachi 3:5-12, telling you how you are going to get paid and how your promotions will work. "⁵And I will come near to you to judgment; and I will be a swift witness against the sorcerers, and against the adulterers, and against false swearers, and against those that oppress the hireling in his wages, the widow, and the fatherless, and that turn aside the stranger from his right, and fear not me, saith the LORD of hosts.⁶For I am the LORD, I change not; therefore ye sons of Jacob are not consumed. ⁷Even from the days of your fathers ye are gone away from mine ordinances, and have not kept them. Return unto me, and I will return unto you, saith the LORD of hosts. But ye said, Wherein shall we return? ⁸Will a man rob God? Yet ye have robbed me. But ye say, Wherein have we robbed thee? In tithes and offerings.⁹Ye are cursed with a curse: for ye have robbed me, even this whole nation. ¹⁰Bring ye all the tithes into the storehouse, that there may be meat in mine house, and prove me now herewith, saith the LORD of hosts, if I will not open you the windows of heaven, and pour you out a blessing, that there shall not be room enough to receive it. ¹¹And I will rebuke the devourer for your sakes, and he shall not destroy the fruits of your ground; neither shall your vine cast her fruit before the time in the field, saith the LORD of hosts. ¹²And all nations shall call you blessed: for ye shall be a delightsome land, saith the LORD of hosts."

Are You Listening Moment: This benefit plan just goes on and on! God talks about it in so many places in the Bible. You've just read quite a bit about it. So what will you do to make sure you get these benefits?

Someone Is Speaking Moment: God is telling you about your life plan (from the beginning, all the way through to your retirement plan) in Psalm 23:1-6. "[1]The LORD is my shepherd; I shall not want.[2]He maketh me to lie down in green pastures: he leadeth me beside the still waters.[3]He restoreth my soul: he leadeth me in the paths of righteousness for his name's sake.[4]Yea, though I walk through the valley of the shadow of death, I will fear no evil: for thou art with me; thy rod and thy staff they comfort me.[5]Thou preparest a table before me in the presence of mine enemies: thou anointest my head with oil; my cup runneth over.[6]Surely goodness and mercy shall follow me all the days of my life: and I will dwell in the house of the LORD forever."

Are You Listening Moment: Did you hear God say he is your shepherd and that you shall not want for anything? We've discussed this point earlier in this book, but I pause here just to remind you of it. That's because it's a pretty big deal. God will look out for you, if you let him. He can restore you and he can build you up, no matter how low you feel or how often you've fallen. He can even lift you up before your enemies, or those who don't like you. That's pretty cool, huh? Think about it. If you have any people at school who have been giving you a hard time, then you can let God handle it. No matter how hard they try to tear you down, he can lift you back up. Trust him to do that, no matter what you are going through. So the next time someone tries to drag you down or hurt you, pray to God and look to him for your answer, help, and protection.

God blesses us all the times. Sometimes we take them for granted or we don't even recognize them. So let's pause to think about just how much God is already blessing us and looking out for us.

List the blessings that God has given you automatically without you even having to ask him:
Example: Air to breathe

1.

2.

3.

4.

5.

6.

7.

8.

9.

10.

Chapter Three

Know Why You Should Give Tithes

Having financial problems? Do you always have to borrow money from family members, friends, loan companies, loan sharks? Do you never seem to have enough money to last through to the end of the month?

Well, look no further. The answers to your money problems can be found right here in this package.

The guidance counselor tells us that we can't solve our financial woes if we don't know where our money is going and how it is working for us.

Your money works for you in a positive way or it will work for you in a negative way. You see, money has no impurity nor does it have prudence. It has no directions nor does it know directions. It has no good sense. It has no forethought, nor does it have discretion. It has no sense of carefulness, or of recklessness; it has no sense of **color or pigmentation**. Money has no preference for who spends it, whether it is male or female. Money likes all individuals.

Money works on a principle

Remember the guidance counselor was speaking over in Malachi 3:6-12: "[6]For I am the LORD, I change not; therefore ye sons of Jacob are not consumed. [7]Even from the days of your fathers ye are gone away from mine ordinances, and have not kept them. Return unto me, and I will return unto you, saith the LORD of hosts. But ye said, Wherein shall we return? [8]Will a man rob God? Yet ye have robbed me. But ye say, Wherein have we robbed thee? In tithes and offerings. [9]Ye are cursed with a curse: for ye have robbed me, even this whole nation. [10]Bring ye all the tithes into the storehouse, that there may be meat in mine house, and prove now herewith, saith the LORD of hosts, if I will not open you the windows of heaven, and pour you out a blessing, that there shall not be room enough to receive it. [11]And I will rebuke the devourer for your sakes, and he shall not destroy the fruits of your ground; neither shall your vine cast her fruit before the time in the field, saith the LORD of hosts. [12]And all nations shall call you blessed: for ye shall be a delightsome land, saith the LORD of hosts."

Are You Listening Moment: As you can see from this passage, giving tithes is important. Tithing is a sign of obedience and being disciplined. When you are obedient to God in this way, he pours out blessings upon you. He asks for the First Fruit.

Christians who give Tithes regularly gives First Fruit. First Fruit is for the disciplined, mature Christian. Only you know if you will give First Fruit. First Fruit requires you to be disciplined, to be able to give.

First Fruit is the first occurrence before any others in a series, preceding or coming ahead of any others in order. It is something that has not been done before or has not occurred before and is best in quality or achievement.

When you give First Fruit to God — it means to give him what you receive first and best in quality.

Example:

When you start your job for the first time and you receive your first paycheck that is First Fruit. Your first paycheck is to be given to God (Yes, which means the whole paycheck) as First Fruit. That is what it means first occurring before any others in a series, or preceding or ahead of any others in an order.

When you get your second paycheck that is when you give God his tithes and offering. (Yes, that means you give God 10 percent of the gross from your second check and an offering).

Then you continue to give God his tithes and offering as long as you receive your paycheck.

Example:

How you give First Fruit when you get a pay raise.

When you get a pay raise, let's say they give you a 4 percent pay raise. You are already making $18 an hour. Now, that you have been given a 4 percent pay raise you now make $18.72.

To Give God His First Fruit, You Do the Following:

You work 40 hours a week. You get paid every two weeks. So you get paid for 80 hours. Therefore, you multiply your 72 cents increase by 80 hours.

Your First Fruit is $57.60 — (.72 x80 =57.60) Give this amount.

First Fruit from pay raise — $57.60

Your tithes — $149.76

Your offering — $15

Your offering is what you decide to give God.

(I suggest that you give God 10 percent of your tithes as an offering.)

What happens when I get my income tax back? Give God 10 percent of your income tax refund.

Example:

Income tax refund — $5,000. Give God $500 as a tithe and $50 offering or double the offering and give $100.

Then you continue to give God his tithes and offering as long as you receive your paycheck.

How to Give God His Tithes:

Example:

Let's say you earn $18 an hour and your gross is $1440 for 80 hours.

You work 40 hours a week. You get paid every two weeks. So you get paid for 80 hours. Therefore, you multiply your gross income $1440 x 10 percent.

Your tithe is $144.

Your offering is a free will offering (what you decide to give God).

Also, another type of offering is **seed offering**.

A **seed offering** is when you give God an offering toward what you are believing him for. If you are praying for a house, give a seed offering every Sunday of any amount and say, "Lord, this is my seed offering toward that house I am believing you for."

Also, "Lord, I will give you so-and-so if what I have prayed for materializes." A good example was Hannah. She prayed for a son and dedicated him to the Lord.

It is just like putting something on lay-a-way. You are putting down small amounts of instalments until you have received the item or items.

Just like God set up the tithing system for you to prosper, he also set up a guide for you to follow each day of your life.

This guide is called the life syllabus (Bible): It would answer the following questions that would come to your mind.

Someone Is Speaking Moment: God says over in Genesis 8:22 that "While the earth remaineth, **seedtime**

and harvest, and cold and heat, and summer and winter, and day and night shall not cease."

Are You Listening Moment: What you plant is what you will receive in seedtime and harvest.

If you give tithes (plant) the windows of heaven will be open unto you. If you plant good seeds you will receive good seeds.

If you plant bad seeds you will receive bad seeds.

You should be very careful of what you plant....Hmm. Hmm. Hmm.

Chapter Four

Know Your Life Plans in Christ Jesus

Sometimes worry and doubt team up to make us all a bit afraid. That fear robs us of our joy. It can even cause us to make poor decisions. And it can prevent us from listening to God's voice.

But you don't have to live like that. Check out this section to show you how to deal with negativity.

GOD HAS A POSITIVE ANSWER

You say: "I'm not smart enough."
God says: "I give you wisdom."
Bible verse: I Corinthians 1:30

You say: "I can't do it."
God says: "You can do all things."
Bible verse: Philippians 4:13

You say: "I'm afraid."
God says: "I have not given you a spirit of fear."
Bible verse: 2 Timothy 1:7

You say: "I can't go on."
God says: "My grace is sufficient."
Bible verses: 2 Corinthians 12:9 & Psalm 91:15

You say: "Nobody really loves me."
God says: "I love you."
Bible verses: John 3:1 6 & John 3:34

You say: "I can't figure things out."
God says: "I will direct your steps."
Bible verses: Proverbs 3:5- 6 & II Corinthians 9:8

You say: "It's not worth it."
God says: "It will be worth it."
Bible verse: Roman 8:28

You say: "I can't forgive myself."
God says: "I forgive you."
Bible verses: I John 1:9 & Romans 8:1

You say: "I can't manage."
God says: "I will supply all your needs."
Bible verse: Philippians 4:19

You say: "I am always worried and frustrated."
God says: "Cast all your cares on ME."
Bible verse: 1 Peter 5:7

You say: "I feel all alone."
God says: "I will never leave you or forsake you."
Bible verse: Hebrews 13:5

You say: "I'm too tired."
God says: "I will give you rest."
Bible verses: Matthew 11:28-30
    Stay with the Life Syllabus (Bible) and you shall
have what you say.

You can even break the Life Syllabus down into steps to follow.

Life Syllabus

Life Syllabus <u>Step One</u> — Believe His Word

If he says it then believe it. Never believe anything that is contrary to his word. So believe and have faith that you have received what you have prayed for.

A lot of Christians pray for something and never expect answers to their prayers. They just pray as a way of life, as a habit, never expecting anything to happen. Some churches or denominations have even formalized prayers, limiting the power of the Holy Spirit to help with our prayers. They just recite the prayers every Sunday. Such prayers never go beyond the roof. So pray and believe for answers to your prayers.

Hebrews 11:13 says: "These all died in faith, not having received the promises, but having seen them afar off, and were persuaded of them, and embraced them, and confessed that they were strangers and pilgrims on earth."

They had faith. They believed even though they had not received the answer. "They were hoping and expecting. Amen! They had no doubt at all that God would do what he promised and what they prayed for. They didn't look at circumstances. They looked beyond circumstances to the One who has promised.

Recently I was reading about Elisha, the prophet, and what he told the king of Israel in the face of severe famine in Israel, and due to Samaria being besieged by the Syrian army. There was severe inflation that resulted in cannibalism, and Elisha told the king that by this time tomorrow a measure of fine flour would be sold for a shekel.

Wow! It is like a gallon of gas going up to $20, and a prophet coming along and saying by this time tomorrow the gallon of gas will sell for $1 per gallon. How many would believe him? But Elisha looked beyond the circumstances around him, the situation around him; to the big God he served--the God of impossibilities, the God who is able to do all things. Elisha believed it, and he received it.

Wow! What a mighty God we serve! We should take our eyes off our situations and focus on Jesus and his Word and promises.

2 Kings 7:1-2 & 16: "Then Elisha said, hear ye the Word of the Lord, thus saith the Lord, tomorrow about this time shall a measure of fine flour be sold for a shekel, and two measures of barley for a shekel, in the gate of Samaria. Then a lord on whose hand the king leaned answered the man of God, and said, behold if the Lord would make windows in heaven, might this thing be? And he said, behold, thou shalt see it with thine eyes, but shalt not eat thereof. And the people went out, and spoiled the tents of the Syrians.

"So a measure of fine flour was sold for a shekel and two measures of barley for a shekel, according to the Word of the Lord."

I was surprised when I read in Luke 8:43 about a woman having an **issue** of **blood** for twelve years. She had spent all her living on physicians, but could not be healed.

So why is it that one Christian prays and receives while another prays and never receives?

This same woman in Mark 5:25 who had an **issue** of **blood** twelve years; only heard about Jesus coming to town and believed for her healing. Over in Luke 8:44 the same woman came behind him (Jesus), and touched the border of his garment: and immediately her **issue** of **blood** stanched.

This proves that there are steps or guidelines to follow. First, you must believe. Second, you must be born again by the Spirit of God into the family of God. You must have committed your life to Jesus Christ.

Life Syllabus <u>Step Two</u> — Act on the Word

Acting on the Word, put your faith into action if you believe it. Then be expectant. Act on what you have prayed for and believe. A lot of Christians miss it here. The problem may not be believing it but putting it into action. Let's look once again at James 2:26. It says: "For as the body without the spirit is dead, so faith without works is dead also."

So put your faith into action.

I gave the example of the woman with the issue of blood. who believed she had received her healing, even though she had not seen the manifestation of that healing. She put her faith into action by getting out of bed and going where Jesus was and was instantly healed.

Another example of putting faith into action is if you believe God for the blessing of the womb, (baby) pray and believe. Start wearing maternity dresses and start buying things for the baby.

The Bible says you should start calling those things that are not as though they were. Start thanking God for a baby or babies. Start confessing it and be expectant. Let your action say to the Lord, "I believe you have answered my prayer. Thank you, Lord."

Life Syllabus <u>Step Three</u> — See It and Visualize it

This is seeing or imagining or dreaming the manifestation of what you have prayed for. Example: If you are a young couple wanting to start a family, see yourself with your inner eyes receiving what you have prayed. See yourself pregnant, with big tummy. See your child running in the house shouting, "Mommy! Mommy! Daddy! Daddy!" If you pray for a car, see yourself driving that car. Joseph dreamed his brothers were bowing down to him. He never forgot that dream.

Let's look at another scripture, Jeremiah 1:11-12:

"Moreover the word of the Lord came unto me, saying, Jeremiah, What seest thou? And I said I see a rod of an almond tree. Then said the Lord unto me, Thou hast well seen: for I will hasten my Word to perform it.

Imagine it, dream it, and see it until it materializes. (Isaiah 62:7) Many things I dreamed about or saw with my inner eyes are now materializing. Example: A pastor who is praying and believing his church to be full every Sunday is doing this. He is seeing and imagining every seat to be occupied. Now this idea is happening, materializing, and he begins looking for a bigger building.

It may look like it is not happening but keep believing it and it shall be so.

Someone Is Speaking Moment: God says in his word in the life syllabus over in Isaiah 62:7, "And give him no rest, (God) till he establish, and till he make Jerusalem a praise in the earth."

God continues to say in Isaiah 55:11 "So shall my (God) word be that goeth forth out of my (God) mouth: it shall not return unto me void, but it shall accomplish that which I please, and it shall prosper in the thing whereto I sent it."

Are You Listening Moment: God shows us over and over just how serious he is about keeping his Word. God reminds us that his words shall not return unto him void. God tells us that his words shall accomplish that which he please and shall prosper in the things whereto he sends it.

Life Syllabus <u>Step Four</u> — Speak It

This is where I sometimes miss it.

Speak the answer. Never say anything negative about what you have prayed for. A lot of people miss it here! Many times pastors say this is a big church, but sometimes pastors find themselves telling people it is a small church. **Always speak** what you have prayed for. Many have been praying and fasting for something, but immediately after they get up they start speaking negatively. Somebody says, "How do you feel?" They reply negatively, "Oh, it is still the same. I don't feel better." Or "It is getting worse." That is negative.

Speak positively. Speak the answer like you have received it. "How do you feel now?" "I feel okay. I am healed in Jesus' name." A business owner or car salesman is being asked a question. Listen to the responses: "How is your business?" "Oh, the business is doing fine."

Never use the words slow, weak, or barely. If you do, you have just negated what you have been praying for.

Always speak the answer like you have received it, even though you cannot physically see it. Keep confessing it until it has manifested. When you pray about something, don't speak against it.

Speak the Word of God like God speaks; the God kind of faith. **Speak like Jesus speaks.** Whatever we speak in the name of Jesus shall be done.

When they told Jesus a child was dead he immediately said, "She is not dead but sleeping; only believe." Amen! They were all laughing at him knowing full well that the child was dead. Was Jesus lying? No. He just refused to speak negatively. When you speak negatively, you have just nullified and cancelled what you have been praying for, so nothing happens.

I saw a Christian in my clinic one day. Everything she said from the beginning to the end was negative, and she painted the sickness so beautifully. She said, "I am a young woman in an old body. Oh, my back is killing me." That back will kill you eventually if you keep saying that. So I told her, "Well you just said it, you get what you say."

Remember: Seedtime and harvest, you will have whatever you plant. People often say, "Say it. It will make you feel better." No! It doesn't!

Words are powerful so be careful what you say. If somebody tells you, you're stupid, cancel it immediately by saying, "I am not stupid."

That is why when I pray for the sick, I always tell them to keep confessing their healing by saying "By his stripes I am healed." The more pain, the more you should confess it. Don't say anything negative. Just keep confessing the Word. Abraham knew this.
Let's look at another scripture in Romans 4:17, 20-21:

"As it is written, I have made thee a father of many nations, before him whom he believed, even God, who quickeneth the dead, and calleth those things which be not as though they were. He staggered not at the promise of God through unbelief; but was strong in faith, giving glory to God; and being fully persuaded that, what He had promised, He was able also to perform.

God called those things that be not as though they were:

Those things were not in existence, but God called them into existence."

Let's have the God kind of faith and speak as God speaks. God's words are powerful.

Hebrews 4:12

"For the **Word of God** is quick, and powerful, and **sharper** than any two edged sword, piercing even to the dividing asunder of soul and spirit, and of the joints and marrow, and is a discerner of the thoughts and intents of the heart."

He said, "Let there be light," and so it was. Our words should also be powerful.

We should say what God says:

Isaiah 55:11

"11So shall my word be that goeth forth out of my mouth: it shall not return unto me void, but it shall accomplish that which I please, and it shall prosper in the thing whereto I sent it."

Just say what God says and angels will move on your behalf. Angels move when we speak positively and demons move when we speak negatively. Powerful words of faith are always positive.

Also, always pray the answer.

Jesus said, "Lazarus come forth." Jesus did not beat around the bush. He prayed the answer.

Life Syllabus <u>Step Five</u> — Thank God

Let's look at Job 22:27-28:

"Thou shalt make thy prayer unto him, and he shall hear thee, and thou shall pay the vows. Thou shall also decree a thing, and it shall be established unto thee; and the light shall shine upon thy ways.

This step is mainly thanking God and praising him.

Praising him for what he has done for you. Thank him and praise him. Bombard heaven with your praises and thanksgiving. I have learned to praise him and thank him for everything I receive whether great or small. He is the source. Thank him profusely. He loves it. He indwells the praises of his people. Give him a thanksgiving offering for what he has done.

Someone Is Speaking Moment: God says give him praise in Psalm 150:1-6. He says, "Praise ye the Lord, Praise God in his sanctuary: praise him in the firmament of his power. Praise him for his mighty acts; praise him according to his excellent greatness. Praise him with the sound of the trumpet: praise him with the psaltery and harp. Praise him with the timbrel and dance: praise him with stringed instruments and organs. Praise him upon the loud cymbals: praise him upon the high sounding cymbals. Let everything that hath breath praise the Lord. Praise ye the Lord."

Are You Listening Moment: When we seek God with an attitude of praise, it opens us up to see, acknowledge, and receive his blessings. Think of three things you want to thank God for today. Say a prayer of thanksgiving, mentioning each thing on your list.

Someone Is Speaking Moment: Proverbs 4:20-22 "My son, attend to my words; incline thine ear unto my sayings. Let them not depart from thine eyes; keep them in the midst of thine heart for they are life unto those that find them, and health to all their flesh."

Jeremiah 1:12 "Then said the Lord unto me, thou hast well seen, for I will hasten my word to perform it."

II Timothy1:7 "For God has not given us the spirit of fear but of power, and of love and of a sound mind."

II Thessalonians 3:3 "But the Lord is faithful, who shall stablish you, and keep you from evil."

Are You Listening Moment: God tells us we must listen. How can you better practice listening to God's Word?

You must remember to give God his words back to him. You must remember to listen for him to answer you back once you have spoken to him.

Just because you have to wait on the answer does not mean that God is not going to answer you. God always answers.

I like what I am hearing!!!
I like what I am hearing!!!
I like what I am hearing!!!

Someone Is Speaking

Chapter Five

How to Have a Conversation With God

Talk with your guidance counselor (GOD) on a daily basis. This isn't Betty talking. This is God. He actually tells us to seek him out in everything we do.

In fact, God tells us in Philippians 4:6 to be careful for nothing; but in everything by prayer and supplication with thanksgiving let your requests be made known unto God.

You might ask if there is a certain way we should let our requests known to God. Well, I will tell you how I make my requests known to God. I give his words back to him because he said in Isaiah 55:11, "So shall my word be that goeth forth out of my mouth: it shall not return unto me void, but it shall accomplish that which I please, and it shall prosper in the thing whereto I sent it."

God is telling you that his words will not return unto him void, but his words shall accomplish and prosper in the thing whereto he sends them.

Example Prayer

Father in the name of Jesus, this is the day the Lord has made and I will rejoice and be glad in it. I come before you this day to say thank you. Thank you Lord for being my Lord, my master, my savior, my God in whom I will trust. Thank you Lord for being my shepherd and supplying all of my needs according to your riches in Glory by Christ Jesus. Thank you Lord. You are an awesome God. Thank you Lord, you are a mighty God. You are my God and I will praise you. You are my God and I will call upon your name. Lord, I thank you for giving me the desires of my heart.

Thank you Lord for opening up the windows of heaven unto me and pouring me out a blessing that I do not have room enough to receive it. Thank you Lord for rebuking the devourer, and not letting him destroy the fruits of my ground. Thank you Lord for it is you God who forgiveth all mine iniquities; as you said in Psalm 103:3. Thank you Lord for it is you God who healeth all (not some) of mine diseases. Thank you Lord for it is you God who sendeth your word, and healeth me, and delivered me from my destructions.

Thank you Lord for your son Jesus for surely he hath borne my grief and carried my sorrows…Thank you Lord for Jesus. He was wounded for my transgressions, he was bruised for my iniquities; the chastisement of our peace was upon him and with his stripes we are healed. I am healed. I am healed. I am healed. I thank you Lord for healing me.

How to have a conversation with God and make it personal

Have a conversation with God by inserting your name into the scriptural references to make your talk more personal.

I've inserted my name in my interpretation of the following scriptures, to demonstrate how to do this.

Psalm 32:8 Father in the name of Jesus you told me that I (God) will instruct you (Betty) in the way you (Betty) should go; I (God) will guide you with my eye.

Psalm 32:7 Father in the name of Jesus you told me that you (God) are my (Betty's) hiding place; You (God) shall preserve me (Betty) from trouble; You (God) shall surround me with songs of deliverance.

Selah. Therefore I thank you Lord for Peace in my life. Lord I thank you for building my house from the ground up. Because you said in Psalm if it is not made I (God) will make it for you.

The Bible may have been written a long time ago, but its message applies to your life today. Often, we have specific issues we want to discuss with God, including health, money, image, etc. I will give you some examples of conversations that you might have with God on specific issues, just remember to put your name in the proper place.

Examples:
Healing Confessions are so very important

Healing Confessions

Father in the name of Jesus, you told me to let my request be known unto you. God this is my request. (Philippians 4:6)

I will not die; I will live and declare the works of the Lord (Psalms 118:17)

I am the healed of the Lord (Psalms 107:20)

I call my body whole

I have the mind of Christ

I am the righteousness in Jesus Christ

I call my body healed (Isaiah 53:5)

I am complete in him; by his stripes I am healed.

Father in the name of Jesus you said that your Word would not return unto you void. Isaiah55:6

Prayer for Prosperity and Blessings

These are your words:

Psalm 46:10 "Be still, and know that I am God."

III John 2 "Beloved, I wish above all things that thou mayest prosper and be in health, even as thy soul prospereth."

Psalms 25:20 "O keep my soul, and deliver me, let me not be ashamed for I put my trust in thee."

Proverbs 4:20-22 "My son, attend to my words; incline thine ear unto my sayings. Let them not depart from thine eyes; keep them in the midst of thine heart for they are life unto those that find them, and health to all their flesh."

Jeremiah 1:12 "Then said the Lord unto me, thou hast well seen, for I will hasten my word to perform it."

II Timothy1:7 "For God has not given us the spirit of fear but of power, and of love and of a sound mind."

II Thessalonians 3:3 "But the Lord is faithful, who shall stablish you, and keep you from evil."

Isaiah 53:4a "Surely he hath borne our griefs, and carried our sorrows…"

Isaiah53:5 "But he was wounded for our transgressions, He was bruised for our iniquities; the chastisement of our peace was upon him and with his stripes we are healed."

Matthew 11:23-24 "For verily I say unto you, that whosoever shall say unto this mountain, be thou removed, and be thou cast in to the sea; and shalt not doubt in his heart, but shall believe that those things which he saith shall come to pass; he shall have whatsoever he saith. Therefore I say unto you, what things soever ye desire when ye pray, believe that ye receive them, and ye shall have them." (Read the next verse and make sure all unforgiveness is out of your heart.)

Prayer for Deliverance/Sickness

Dear heavenly father, I come to you to seek deliverance. I know you are my protector. You are my source. For in your Word, you said:

Psalm 103:3 Who forgiveth all thine iniquities; who healeth all (not some) thy diseases.

Psalm 107:20 He sent his word, and healed them, and delivered them from their destructions.

Jeremiah 17:14a Heal me O Lord, and I shall be healed;

Jeremiah 33:6 Behold, I will bring it health and cure, and I will cure them, and will reveal unto them the abundance of peace and truth.

Psalm 30:2 O Lord my God, I cried unto thee, and thou hast healed me

Psalm 34:19 Many are the afflictions of the righteous but the Lord delivereth him out of them all.

Psalm 55:18 He has delivered my soul in peace from the battle that was against me for there were many with me.

Psalm 97:10b …He preserveth the souls of his saints; He delivereth them out of the hand of the wicked.

Isaiah 53:4a Surely he hath borne our griefs, and carried our sorrows.

Isaiah 53:5 But he was wounded for our transgressions, he was bruised for our iniquities; the chastisement of our peace was upon him, and with his stripes we are healed.

Prayer for Peace

Craft a prayer using these scriptures:

I Peter 2:24 Who his own self bare our sins in his own body on the tree, that we being dead to sins, should live unto righteousness; by whose stripes ye were healed

Romans 8:2 For the law of the spirit of life in Christ Jesus hath made me free from the law of sin and death,

Romans 8:32 He that spared not his own son, but delivered him up for us all, how shall he not with him also freely give us all things.

John 14:27 Peace I leave with you, my peace I give unto you not as the world giveth, give I unto you. Let not your heart be troubled, neither Let it be afraid.

I Kings 8:56 Blessed be the Lord, that hath given rest unto his people Israel, according to all that he promised; there hath not failed one word of all his promise, which He promised by the hand of Moses his servant.

Psalm.97:10b...He preserveth the souls of his saints; he delivereth them out of the hand of the wicked.

Philippians 4:7 And the peace of God, which passeth all understanding, shall keep your hearts and minds through Christ Jesus.

John 14:27 Peace I leave with you, my peace I give unto you, not as the world giveth, give I unto you. Let not your heart be troubled, neither let it be afraid. Psalm 46:10 Be still, and know that I am God. I Kings 8:56 Blessed be the Lord, that hath given rest unto his people Israel, according to all that he promised: there hath not failed one word of all his promise, which he promised by the hand of Moses his servant. Jeremiah 1:12 Then said the Lord unto me, thou hast well seen for I will hasten my word to perform it.

Personal Confessions

Psalm 32:8 Father in the name of Jesus you told me that I (God) will instruct you (Betty) in the way you should go; I (God) will guide you with my eye.

Psalm 32:7 Father in the name of Jesus you told me that you (God) are my hiding place; You shall preserve me (Betty) (put your name) from trouble; You shall surround me with songs of deliverance. Selah.

I am quick, I am bright, I am sharp, I am beautiful, I am very rich, I am blessed and highly favored by God, and I am a major blessing,

I am debt-free; I owe no man anything but to love him. I have the mind of Christ.

II Corinthians 2:14a Now thanks be unto God, which always causeth us to triumph in Christ.

Housekeeping/Roommates Confessions

I have a very clean house always, each and every day.
I have a very organized house.
I have a very clean office always, each and every day. I have a very organized office. I am blessed and highly favored by the Lord. I am blessed to live in a nice neighborhood, and I am blessed because God has built me a house. I am blessed to have a house built on three acres of land.

School Confession

Father in the name of Jesus, I want to thank you that you have given me wisdom and knowledge in my studies. Thank you father, that I have interest in the subjects that I must study.

Father in the name of Jesus, I ask that you give me wisdom and knowledge like you gave to Daniel and make me ten times smarter. I pray that you will give me perfect recall and a photographic memory for all of my exams and throughout my studies for the degree that I am pursuing. That I will be able to recall the very pages, even the very paragraph that my answers appear in for each question as needed. God I ask that you do a quick work on my behalf and that I will graduate with honors. I believe that you are able to do exceedingly and abundantly above all that we ask or think, according to the power that worketh inside of me, and even beyond that because you said that you God are able to make all your grace abound to us that need it the most. It is a done deal in Jesus, because you said whatever we ask for in your son Jesus' name it will be done. Amen and Amen.

Money Confessions

Father in the name of Jesus, I thank you that the windows of heaven are open unto me because I have brought all of the tithes and offering according to your Word found in Malachi 3:10.

I do not ever run out of money.
I always have plenty of money.
I shall have plenty of money in my purse, pockets, and bank accounts.
I am debt-free. I owe no man anything but to love him.

Thank You God that you have made me a multimillionaire today.

Father in the name of Jesus, thank you God that you: have already touched someone's heart and told them to bring me a million dollars today. I thank you God that that person has already obeyed your Word and they have brought the million dollars and placed it in my right hand. God I ask that you give it back to them in favors. Because, you said, Betty give and it shall be given back to you, pressed down, shaken together, and running over shall men give into your bosoms. You also said you would supply all of my needs according to your riches in Glory by Christ Jesus. I have God's word on the matter; therefore, I am blessed in the city and in the field.

Image Confessions

Father in the name of Jesus, I do not know why you made me and other individuals in the shapes and sizes that you did (so tall, so short, so big, so fat, so small, large hips, large eyes), but this is what your Word told me. Everything that you made was good, no matter the shape, size, color, or hair length.

My body is whole and strong from the top my head to the soles of my feet. My body is beautiful. By Jesus' stripes I am healed from all manner of sickness and disease.

My body is whole and strong.
I can do anything I want to do.
I can eat anything I want to eat.
I can go anywhere I want to go.

All in the name of Jesus.
Thank you Father for your Word, that I am whole.
Things just flow for me always.
I am blessed and highly favored of the Lord.
Things go well for me all the time;
I have great favor with whomever I come in contact
 with each day of my life.

People Confession/Friendship Confession

Father in the name of Jesus, you told me to make myself friendly. You told me to treat people like I want to be treated, so I'm going to say what your Word told me to say.

People just look at me and like me and they do not even know why. People always want to help me or do something for me and bless me. People see the God in me. People see the peace of God upon me. People see the joy of God in me. People see the favor of God upon my life. People see the light of God upon my face.

I like what I am hearing!!!
I like what I am hearing!!!
I like what I am hearing!!!

Some Is Speaking

Chapter Six

How to Ask God for Things

Everyone has questions. Some people even say that inquiring minds want to know. Well, we have discussed earlier that God said let your request be known unto him over in Philippians 4:17. God has invited you to pose your questions, solicit, and ask over again your concerns. So, once again he says raise your questions, and put your questions on the line.

Someone Is Speaking Moment: Jesus tells you how to ask God for things and how to receive things from God over in John 16:23. "And in that day ye shall **ask me** (Jesus) **nothing**. Verily, verily, I say unto you, what so ever ye shall **ask** the Father in my name, he will give it you."

Are You Listening Moment: Jesus really breaks it down. He says we can ask God anything and God will give it to us, if we ask in the name of Jesus. Seeing this information here does it open up some real possibilities for you? Are you suddenly thinking about all you can ask God for in the name of Jesus? How does this information change your prayer life?

Someone Is Speaking Moment: God tells you how to ask for things from him over in Philippians 4:6. Be careful for nothing; but in everything by prayer and supplication with thanksgiving **let your requests be made known unto God.**

Are You Listening Moment: What God means here is don't hold back. Keep those requests coming to him. Has there been something you've wanted to pray about but you weren't sure God was interested in hearing about it? If so, take even that to him, because he wants to hear about it.

Someone Is Speaking Moment: God tells you what to expect once you have asked him for something over in Philippians 4:7. "And the peace of God, which passeth all understanding, shall keep your hearts and minds through Christ Jesus."

Are You Listening Moment: When you go to God in prayer and make a decision based on his leading and what is in his Word, he will give you peace about that decision. That feeling of peace lets you know you are doing the right thing. Have you ever made a decision and felt at peace about it, even if it was a tough choice?

Someone Is Speaking Moment: God gives you instructions on how to ask and what to expect when you ask him for something over in Philippians 4:9. "Those things, which ye have both learned, and received, and heard, and seen in me, do: and the God of peace shall be with you."

Are You Listening Moment: The Bible is an instruction manual that can help us with any decision we make. If you are struggling with an issue in your life or a decision, open God's Word to see how he addressed a similar issue. Look for the principles in the Bible and use those principles to address what you are going through and you will be on your way to making good decisions. What decision are you facing today?

Someone Is Speaking Moment: The model prayer that God gave us to follow is found in Matthew 6:9-15.
9"After this manner therefore pray ye: Our Father which art in heaven, Hallowed be thy name. 10Thy kingdom come, Thy will be done in earth, as it is in heaven. 11Give us this day our daily bread. 12And forgive us our debts, as we forgive our debtors.13And lead us not into temptation, but deliver us from evil: For thine is the kingdom, and the power, and the glory, forever. Amen. 14For if ye forgive men their trespasses, your heavenly Father will also forgive you: 15But if ye forgive not men their trespasses, neither will your Father forgive your trespasses."

Are You Listening Moment: This is a very simple but powerful prayer. If ever you are in a position where you are not sure what or how to pray, say this prayer.

Someone Is Speaking Moment: God tells us over in Romans 8:26-27, "Likewise the Spirit also helpeth our infirmities: for we know not what we should pray for as we ought: but the Spirit itself maketh **intercession** for us with groanings which cannot be uttered. And he that searcheth the hearts knoweth what is the mind of the Spirit, because he maketh **intercession** for the saints (us) according to the will of God."

Are You Listening Moment: The Holy Spirit works in us to give guidance. Even if you don't know what you should pray for, listen to hear that still, quiet voice urging you. That voice is the Holy Spirit. Have you ever heard the Holy Spirit urging you to do something? How did you respond?

Someone Is Speaking Moment: In Daniel 10:1-20 there is a man by the name of Daniel who prayed and asked God for something. It took 21 days before Daniel heard from God about his prayer. God sent an angel to talk with Daniel to tell him why it took so long for him to hear back from God. This angel told Daniel that he was in a fight and Michael the archangel had to come and help him to fight, just so that Daniel could get his answer from God.

Sometimes things happen and we don't hear back from God immediately, as in Daniel's case. But just know that God does hear each conversation and prayer that you have with him. He will answer you, but it just might take some time.

The Bible has several examples of people who prayed and heard from God — some heard back immediately, while others had to wait a while. There was **Nehemiah**, for instance, who prayed and God answered him the very day that he prayed. In Nehemiah 1:11 Nehemiah, the cupbearer, prayed early one morning and God answered him the very same day. His answer came in Chapter 2.

In the New Testament, there was a man by the name of **Zacharias** who had prayed and asked God to let his wife have a child.

God answered him in Luke 1:13. "But the angel said unto him, Fear not, Zacharias: for thy **prayer** is heard;

and thy wife Elisabeth shall bear thee a son, and thou shalt call his name John."

There was a man by the name of **Samuel** who prayed and asked the Lord to send rain and thunder. In first Samuel 12:17 (Samuel) stated, "Is it not wheat harvest today? I will call unto the LORD, and he shall send thunder and **rain**; that ye may perceive and see that your wickedness is great, which ye have done in the sight of the LORD, in asking you a king."

The Lord heard his prayer and answered him over in first Samuel 12:18, "So Samuel called unto the LORD; and the LORD sent thunder and **rain** that day: and all the people greatly feared the LORD and Samuel."

There was a man by the name of **Elias** who prayed and asked God to send no rain for three years and six months over in James 5:17. "Elias was a man subject to like passions as we are, and he prayed earnestly that it might not **rain**: and it **rain**ed not on the earth by the space of three years and six months."

There was a man named **Joshua** who prayed and asked God to let the sun stand still until he finished fighting his enemy in Joshua 10:12. "Then spake Joshua to the LORD in the day when the LORD delivered up the Amorites before the children of Israel, and he said in the sight of Israel, **Sun**, stand thou still upon Gibeon; and thou, Moon, in the valley of Ajalon."

God heard Joshua's prayer and made the sun and the moon to stand still for him in Joshua 10:13. "And the **sun** stood still, and the moon stayed, until the people had avenged themselves upon their enemies. Is not this written in the book of Jasher? So the **sun** stood still in the midst of heaven, and hasted not to go down about a whole day."

There was a young man by the name of **Jabez** who prayed to God for blessing on his life and asked God to guide him with his hand. God heard his prayer and answered him in the book of 1 Chronicles 4:10. "And **Jabez** called on the God of Israel, saying, Oh that thou wouldest bless me indeed, and enlarge my coast, and that thine hand might be with me, and that thou wouldest keep me from evil, that it may not grieve me! And God granted him that which he requested."

And here is one final example. There was a man by the name of **Hezekiah** who prayed and asked the Lord to extend his life, so that he could live longer.

God answered him in the book of Isaiah 38:5. God said, "Go, and say to Hezekiah, Thus saith the LORD, the God of David thy father, I have heard thy **prayer**, I have seen thy tears: **behold, I will add unto thy days fifteen years.**"

Are You Listening Moment: Is there one particular example here that you especially relate to? Which one of these examples best helps you understand how God answers prayers?

Someone Is Speaking Moment: Just remember what God says in Matthew 21:22, "In all things, whatsoever ye shall ask in **prayer**, believing, ye shall receive."

Are You Listening Moment: Did you see where all those individuals asked God for something and God answered them each and every time?

Did you see where he answered some the same day, where he answered some 21 days later, and some one year later? Have you ever prayed for something and the answer did not come right away but came a while later? How did you respond to that?

Think about some things you seriously need to ask God about now. Write about them.

Improve on your own communications skills with God

Things I want to ask God about:
1.
2.
3.
4.
5.
6.
7.
8.
9.
10.

List at least one scripture that corresponds to each question or thing you want to ask God:
1.
2.
3.
4.
5.
6.
7.
8.
9.
10.

In 3 John 2, you hear God pronounce three blessings over your life. They are:

1. That you may prosper above all things (material blessings, houses, land, cars, etc.)

2. That you may be in health (healed from all manner of sickness, and diseases, yes that means cancer, AIDS, colds, coughs, fevers, etc.)

3. That your soul prospers (healthy mind, healthy thoughts, etc.)

Someone Is Speaking Moment: God tells us over in Ephesians 2:1-10, [1] "And you hath he quickened, who were dead in trespasses and sins; [2]Wherein in time past ye walked according to the course of this world, according to the prince of the power of the air, the spirit that now worketh in the children of disobedience: [3]Among whom also we all had our conversation in times past in the lusts of our flesh, fulfilling the desires of the flesh and of the mind; and were by nature the children of wrath, even as others. 4But God, who is rich in mercy, for his great love wherewith he loved us, 5Even when we were dead in sins, hath quickened us together with Christ, (by grace ye are saved;) 6And hath raised us up together, and made us sit together in heavenly places in Christ Jesus: 7That in the ages to come he might shew the exceeding riches of his grace in his kindness toward us through Christ Jesus. 8For by grace are ye saved through faith; and that not of yourselves: it is the gift of God: 9Not of works, lest any man should boast.10For we are his workmanship, created in Christ Jesus unto good works, which God hath before ordained that we should walk in them."

Are You Listening Moment: More blessings! More blessings! More blessings! Now that you see so many other blessings that God wants to pour into your life, do you feel even more strongly that you want to live according to his will? Is there anything stopping you today from living by everything he says, so you receive these and other blessings? If so, what is that?

I like what I am hearing!!!
I like what I am hearing!!!
I like what I am hearing!!!

Someone Is Speaking

Chapter Seven

What to Expect When You Talk With God

When you expect to hear from God, you are waiting for good news. When you talk with God, have a conversation with God, and even when you pray to God you are in the expecting stage, anticipating good things to happen to you or others. All the while you are telling yourself you are supposed to receive good gifts from your father above, because he told you that you were the apple of his eye and that he would withhold no good thing from you.

So how do we know if our expectation is realistic or if there is more to it than simply wanting good things to happen? Well, as we've done throughout this book, let's look to God's Word to find the answer.

Someone Is Speaking Moment: God tells you what to expect when you talk with him over in Jeremiah 29:11-13. "For I know the thoughts that I think toward you, saith the LORD, thoughts of peace, and not of evil, to give you an expected end.

"Then shall ye call upon me, and ye shall go and pray unto me, and I will hearken unto you.

"And ye shall seek me, and find me, when ye shall search for me with all your heart."

Are You Listening Moment: We see from this that God wants to do good things for us, but notice the condition: He says when we search for him with the whole heart. So praying and wanting good things to happen must be matched with a desire to truly seek God. Now that you've found this out, does that help you understand more fully the spirit you must be in or the attitude you must have when you pray?

Someone Is Listening Moment: God tells us over in Romans 10:9-10, "If you would open up your mouth – that if thou shalt confess with thy mouth the Lord Jesus, and shalt believe in thine heart that God hath raised him from the dead, thou shalt be saved. For with the heart man believeth unto righteousness; and with the mouth confession is made unto salvation."

And Romans 10:13 says, "For whosoever shall call upon the name of the Lord shall be saved."

Are You Listening Moment: Did you hear God tell you to confess with your mouth the Lord Jesus? Then, God told you to believe in your heart that God hath raised him from the dead. Then, God told you that you would be saved. God went on to tell you with your heart believe unto righteousness and with your mouth confession is made unto salvation.

Expecting a certain result from prayer is about believing God's Word. Do you believe God to do for you what he says he will do? Does your life reflect this? If not, what will you change?

Someone Is Speaking Moment: This is what was said when Paul had a conversation with God. Paul wrote to the saints at Ephesus and told them what he had told God that he wanted for them.

Check out **Ephesians 1:1-23.**

"1Paul, an apostle of Jesus Christ by the will of God, to the saints which are at Ephesus, and to the faithful in Christ Jesus:

"2Grace be to you, and peace, from God our Father, and from the Lord Jesus Christ.

"3Blessed be the God and Father of our Lord Jesus Christ, who hath blessed us with all spiritual blessings in heavenly places in Christ:

"4According as he hath chosen us in him before the foundation of the world, that we should be holy and without blame before him in love:

"5Having predestinated us unto the adoption of children by Jesus Christ to himself, according to the good pleasure of his will, "6To the praise of the glory of his grace, wherein he hath made us accepted in the beloved.

"7In whom we have redemption through his blood, the forgiveness of sins, according to the riches of his grace;

"8Wherein he hath abounded toward us in all wisdom and prudence;

"9Having made known unto us the mystery of his will, according to his good pleasure which he hath purposed in himself:

"10That in the dispensation of the fullness of times he might gather together in one all things in Christ, both which are in heaven, and which are on earth; even in him:

"11In whom also we have obtained an inheritance, being predestinated according to the purpose of him who worketh all things after the counsel of his own will:

"12That we should be to the praise of his glory, who first trusted in Christ.

"13In whom ye also trusted, after that ye heard the word of truth, the gospel of your salvation: in whom also after that ye believed, ye were sealed with that Holy Spirit of promise,

"14Which is the earnest of our inheritance until the redemption of the purchased possession, unto the praise of his glory.

"15Wherefore I also, after I heard of your faith in the Lord Jesus, and love unto all the saints,

"16Cease not to give thanks for you, making mention of you in my prayers;

"17That the God of our Lord Jesus Christ, the Father of glory, may give unto you the spirit of wisdom and revelation in the knowledge of him:

"18The eyes of your understanding being enlightened; that ye may know what is the hope of his calling, and what the riches of the glory of his inheritance in the saints,

"[19]And what is the exceeding greatness of his power to us-ward who believe, according to the working of his mighty power,

"[20]Which he wrought in Christ, when he raised him from the dead, and set him at his own right hand in the heavenly places,

"[21]Far above all principality, and power, and might, and dominion, and every name that is named, not only in this world, but also in that which is to come:

"[22]And hath put all things under his feet, and gave him to be the head over all things to the church,

"[23]Which is his body, the fullness of him that filleth all in all."

Are You Listening Moment: What does this passage make you feel and understand about your prayers, expectation, and what God already has for you?

I like what I am hearing!!!
I like what I am hearing!!!
I like what I am hearing!!!

Someone Is Speaking

Chapter Eight

Your Outer Ears vs. Your Inner Ears

When you listen with your physical ears you hear what the world has to say. You have an outer ear experience. But, when you listen to that still, small voice, the Word of God, you hear what God has to say to you. You have an inner ear experience.

Someone Is Speaking Moment: God tells us over in Isaiah 30:21 "And thine ears shall hear a word behind thee, saying, This is the way, walk ye in it, when ye turn to the right hand, and when ye turn to the left."

Are You Listening Moment: This means you are never alone when you are a child of God. God is with you — he is in you, guiding you at every turn. Have you ever heard God speaking to you but you chose to listen to your friends or others who told you to do something different? What did you learn from that experience?

Someone Is Speaking Moment: God tells us over in John 10:27 "My sheep hear my voice, and I know them, and they follow me:"

God continues to tell us about his sheep (us) in John 10:14, "I am the good shepherd, and know my sheep, and am known of mine."

God tells us how his sheep (us) travel with him in John 10:4. "And when he putteth forth his own sheep, he goeth before them, and the sheep follow him: for they know his voice."

Are You Listening Moment: As you begin studying the Bible more and listening to what God has to say, you will become more aware of his voice. You will be able to hear him very clearly.

Someone Is Speaking Moment: God tells us over in Proverbs 3:6, "In all thy ways acknowledge him, and he shall direct thy paths."

Are You Listening Moment: This means live your life according to what you think will please God. You are then acknowledging his guidance and following his direction. Can you make one change today to begin living your life in this way?

Someone Is Speaking Moment: God tells us over in Psalm 37:23, "The steps of a good man are ordered by the Lord and he delighteth in his way."

Are You Listening Moment: You can tell if someone is listening to that still, small voice by what you see in that person's life. What do people see in your life?

Someone Is Speaking Moment: God tells us over in Romans 12: 3, "For I say, through the grace given unto me, to every man that is among you, not to think of himself more highly than he ought to think; but to think soberly, according as God hath dealt to every man the measure of faith."

Are You Listening Moment: When things are going well for us, sometimes it's easy to become a little arrogant and think that we are the ones actually making things happen. But this passage cautions us against thinking more highly of ourselves than we should. So try to always seek out God, even when you feel that you don't need him or that you are doing quite all right on your own.

Have you ever been feeling really good about how well you've done something that you became a bit too proud or arrogant? What was the result?

God continues to speak to us about faith over in Romans 10:17 he says so then faith cometh by hearing, and hearing by the word of God.

Gods says that everyone has access to faith, everyone can hear the Word of God, and that it is up to each individual to accept the Word of God.

Someone Is Speaking Moment: God reminds us over in Proverbs 16:9, "A man's heart deviseth his way: but the Lord directeth his steps."

Are You Listening Moment: Have you been letting God direct your steps? How can you tell?

Someone Is Speaking Moment: God tells us in Isaiah 42:16, "And I (God) will bring the blind by a way that they knew not; I (God) will lead them in the paths that they have not known: I will make darkness light before them, and crooked things straight. These things will I do unto them, and not forsake them."

Are You Listening Moment: If you choose to listen with your inner ears, God will lead you and show you a way you didn't even know anything about! That means he can even show you how to accomplish your goals and dreams in a way you were not even aware existed. If you've been struggling with doing a certain thing — whether it's passing a certain class, advancing in a certain career, or even growing a certain business — try to start listening to God with your inner ears and see what answers he provides.

Someone Is Speaking Moment: God tells us in Psalm 73:23-24: "Nevertheless I (God) am continually with thee' thou hast holden me by my right hand. Thou shalt guide me with thy counsel, and afterward receive me to glory."

Are You Listening Moment: All of this boils down to a very simple concept: God will speak to us, and it is left up to us to hear him and obey.

Someone Is Speaking Moment: God did tell us over in John 15:1-5, "I (God) am the true vine and my father is the husbandman. Every branch in me that beareth not fruit he taketh away; and every branch that beareth fruit, he purgeth it, that it may bring forth more fruit. Now ye are clean through the word which I have spoken unto you. Abide in me, and I in you. As the branch cannot bear fruit of itself, except it abide in the vine; no more can ye, except ye abide in me. I am the vine, ye are the branches: He that abideth in me, and I in him, the same bringeth forth much fruit for without me ye can do nothing."

Are You Listening Moment: What this means is the only real way to produce good fruit is to pay attention to that inner voice and live in God. Are you ready to do that?

Someone Is Speaking Moment: God says in Psalm 1:3, "And he shall be like a tree planted by the rivers of water, that bringeth forth his fruit in his season; his leaf also shall not wither; and whatsoever he doeth shall prosper."

Are You Listening Moment: When you feed on the Word of God, you will prosper. Are you consuming — reading, listening to, discussing — God's Word on a regular basis? If not, are you ready to start?

Someone Is Speaking Moment: God says that it does not stop there. He tells us in Psalm 92:14, "They shall still bring forth fruit in old age; they shall be fat and flourishing;…"

Are You Listening Moment: Once you hook up with God (your guidance counselor), you have the hook-up of a lifetime.

Someone Is Speaking Moment: God explains this beautiful lifetime hook-up in **Psalm 1:1-6** "1Blessed is the man that walketh not in the counsel of the ungodly, nor standeth in the way of sinners, nor sitteth in the seat of the scornful.

"2But his delight is in the law of the LORD; and in his law doth he meditate day and night.

"3And he shall be like a tree planted by the rivers of water, that bringeth forth his fruit in his season; his leaf also shall not wither; and whatsoever he doeth shall prosper.

"4The ungodly are not so: but are like the chaff which the wind driveth away. 5Therefore the ungodly shall not stand in the judgment, nor sinners in the congregation of the righteous.

"6For the LORD knoweth the way of the righteous: but the way of the ungodly shall perish."

God talks with you in Romans 12:2 "2And be not conformed to this world: but be ye transformed by the renewing of your mind, that ye may prove what is that good, and acceptable, and perfect, will of God."

Are You Listening Moment: When you transform your mind, it means you change the way you think. You no longer think like the world, but you think like God. You view your life from a spiritual standpoint and you draw closer to that still, small voice.

The following exercise helps you see the difference between what you might hear with your outer (worldly) ears and your inner (Godly) ears.

List the things you hear with your outer ears.
Example: Stay out late and party. Do not do your class assignments. Do not respect your elders. Do not pay your bills on time. Do not show up for your appointments on time. Do not return your books to the library on time, etc.

1.
2.
3.
4.
5.

List the things that you would hear with your inner ear.

Example: Obey your parents. Do not do evil for evil.
1.
2.
3.
4.
5.
6.
7.
8.
9.
10.

List the things that you would like to hear from your Guidance Counselor (God).

Example: Matthew 25: 23
Matthew 25:23 **His** lord said unto him, **Well done**, good and faithful servant; thou hast been faithful over a few things, I will make thee ruler over many things: enter thou into the joy of thy lord.
1.
2.
3.
4.
5.

I like what I am hearing!!!
I like what I am hearing!!!
I like what I am hearing!!!

Someone Is Speaking

Chapter Nine

The Voice Behind the Scriptures

God will always be the voice behind the scriptures. Many people discount the Bible because they say it was written by men and that men make mistakes. But this is wrong thinking. While men may have penned the words, the scriptures came through divine inspiration. God spoke to those Biblical writers and passed down thoughts, ideas, and principles that have stood the test of time.

The principles God gave still apply today, thousands of years after the words were written. So don't think the Bible does not apply to you. When you understand the voice behind the scriptures, you realize the Bible is as relevant today as it was then.

We will study this here:

Someone Is Speaking Moment: God tells us in Deuteronomy 7:9, "Know therefore that the Lord thy God, he is God, the faithful God, which keepeth covenant and mercy with them that love him and keep his commandments to a thousand generations;..."

Are You Listening Moment: This passage helps us understand who God is. He is faithful and merciful to those who love him.

This is who cared so much for us that he gave us an entire instruction book called the Bible. What is your opinion of God from what you've read in the Bible? When you think of God, you think what exactly?

Someone Is Speaking Moment: God tells us over in Deuteronomy 4:31, "(For thy Lord thy God is a merciful God;) he will not forsake thee, neither destroy thee, nor forget the covenant of thy fathers which he sware unto them."

Are You Listening Moment: This is more evidence of God's character. What does this tell you about God?

Someone Is Speaking Moment: God tells us in Psalm 105:8, "He (God) hath remembered his covenant for ever, the word which he commanded to a thousand generations."

Are You Listening Moment: This means God keeps his Word. He is not like some of those around us who tell us one thing but then do another. We can trust God. How does that make you feel?

Someone Is Speaking Moment: God tells us about his faithfulness over in Numbers 23:19, "God is not a man, that he should lie; neither the son of man, that he should repent: hath he said, and shall he not do it? Or hath he spoken, and shall he not make it good?"

Are You Listening Moment: God makes it clear that if he says something, he is good for it. Who is the person you trust most in your life? Now, think about this: You can trust God even more than that person. That's pretty cool, huh?

Someone Is Speaking Moment: God lets us know in Hebrews 10:23 that we can rely on the words that he has given us. The Word says, "Let us hold fast the profession of our faith without wavering; (for he is faithful that promised)."

Are You Listening Moment: God wants us to trust him so much that he spent quite a lot of time assuring us he can be trusted. This passage is just one of many that let us know God is faithful. So do you believe it?

Someone Is Speaking Moment: God tells us in 2 Peter 3:9, "The Lord is not slack concerning his promise, as some men count slackness; but is longsuffering to us-ward,…"

Are You Listening Moment: God has said it again. He can be trusted.

Someone Is Speaking Moment: Psalm 9:10 says, "And they that know thy name will put their trust in thee (God); for thou, Lord, has not forsaken them that seek thee."

Are You Listening Moment: When you get to know God, you too will trust him. He will never let you down. Does this passage give you an even clearer idea of who God, the voice behind the scriptures, is?

Someone Is Speaking Moment: God says in Isaiah 54:10, "For the mountains shall depart, and the hills be removed; but my kindness shall not depart from thee neither shall the covenant of my peace be removed saith the Lord that hath mercy on them."

Are You Listening Moment: That's a pretty big promise! The very surface of the earth may pass away, but God's promises to you will not.

By now, if you are like me, you may be so excited about the promises God has made to us that you are ready to share this Word with everyone who will listen! I know I am so excited. That's why I wrote this book.

Maybe you want to tell Hollywood, and get a studio to make this story into a movie. Maybe you want to tell New York, and get more authors to turn these words into books. Maybe you want to tell… Well, just tell everyone you can.

John 21:15-17 puts it this way, "So when they had dined, Jesus saith to Simon Peter, 'Simon, son of Jonas, lovest thou me more than these?' He saith unto him, 'Yea, Lord; thou knowest that I love thee.' He saith unto him, 'Feed my lambs.' He saith to him (Simon Peter) again the second time, 'Simon, son of Jonas, lovest thou me?' He saith unto him, 'Yea, Lord; thou knowest that I love thee.' He saith unto him, 'Feed my sheep.' He saith unto him the third time, 'Simon, son of Jonas, lovest thou me?' Peter was grieved because he said unto him the third time, 'Lovest thou me?' And he said unto him, 'Lord, thou knowest all things; thou knowest that I love thee.' Jesus saith unto him, 'Feed my Sheep.'"

So we too must feed the sheep. We must tell others about what we have learned about God and his plan for our lives. The following exercise will help you begin telling others about God today.

I will share this good news with the following people:
1.
2.
3.
4.
5.
6.
7.
8.
9.
10.

I like what I am hearing!!!
I like what I am hearing!!!
I like what I am hearing!!!

Someone Is Speaking

Chapter Ten

Stages of Faith

The stages of faith are like human life. The first stage is like being a newborn. A newborn baby is in the infant stage, and then develops to the toddler stage, preschool stage, elementary stage, junior high school stage, high school stage, college stage, graduate school stage, and last but not least, life stage.

When the gospel of the Kingdom is preached, the Holy Spirit bears witness to the hearer. So it is with your faith walk, to move from one stage of faith to the next stage of faith. There are baby Christians and there are mature Christians. The more you use the Word of God (faith), believe the Word of God and accept God at his word, the stronger your faith becomes.

The "life coach" assignment has been to train converts (Christians) for the work of the Kingdom. The church receives the new believer in his natural state and nurtures him/her through his carnal state, on to maturity.

The church has within its body believers who are experiencing different stages in their lives. All are at some stage, which is a different place from the others, but they are all in the one body of Christ.

Christians have different stages that they must go through just like you have different classes that you must take in order to graduate from high school.

The different levels of spiritual maturity of believers in the church place each individual in a growth mode or different stage at all times. The goal for each believer is transformation from the fleshly nature to the God kind of nature, the living nature.

Just like it takes you twelve years combined to complete grade school and high school, it takes time for the believer, the Christian, to mature in the Word of God.

Right now you are getting ready to enter into the University Stage of your life.

For the Christians they too must enroll into a university:
- The University of Death — When you come out of the womb
- The University of Hard Knocks — Just going through life
- The University of Straddling the Fence-Heard about Jesus/not ready
- The University of Life — Have accepted Jesus as Lord and Savior
- Graduate School — Leading others to Christ
- The University of Eternal Life — Have a home in heaven

Someone Is Speaking Moment: Romans 6:23 say, "For the wages of **sin is death**, but **the gift of God is eternal life** through Jesus Christ our Lord."

Are You Listening Moment: Did you hear God say that when you choose him, Jesus Christ, you will receive eternal life? When you choose to sin, it will bring death.

Someone Is Speaking Moment: God is speaking in Deuteronomy 30:19, "I call heaven and earth to record this day against you that I have set before you life and death, blessing and cursing: therefore **choose life**, that both thou and thy seed may live."

Are You Listening Moment: And that is the point of this entire book: God is speaking and asking you to choose life. So do that. Choose life, so that you may live.

Based on all you have read in this book, are you ready to listen with your whole heart to what God is saying? Will you choose life?

Just Remember ...

Someone Is Speaking: Are You Listening?

Someone Is Speaking: Are you Listening?

Response

Referring to God as Our Guidance Counselor in my Book, "Someone Is Speaking: Are you Listening?", prompts me the Author and hopefully prompts you the Reader to actually Stop and Listen to God who is speaking to us through his anointed Word.

It is my sincere heartfelt desire for the readers of this book to know that God has commanded us in 2nd Timothy to:
Study *to shew thyself approved unto God, a workman that needeth not to be ashamed, rightly dividing the word of truth.*

As a result of studying God's word we found God's wish for us over in III John 2 *Beloved, I wish above all things that thou mayest prosper and be in health, even as thy soul prospereth..*

Individual/Student Response: That is so cool, really cool. Ok, ok, ok. Now I understand, and once everyone else gets the understanding, that it was God who has their itinerary already made for life, they will have the God kind of life too.
Given the right environment, I feel that we all can be winners, as long as we follow the life plan that God has established for us. Everyone cannot be doctors and lawyers, we need people who can cook, sew, paint, wash, teach etc., so we all can be complete.
We complete each other.

About the Author

Betty Allen, a native of Louisiana, is the wife of Tony Britton. She accepted her gift to be a writer and inspirational and motivational speaker at the tender age of twelve.

Those who know Betty and cross her path see her as quiet and very soft-spoken. But, she is on fire for the things of the Lord. She has an ever-burning desire to study the Word of God and apply it to her daily life.

This book is a result of Betty listening to a well-known minister (life coach) from Dallas, Texas on New Year's Eve 2010 via the Internet. The message preached assured that yet another woman would be loosed.

Back Cover

Someone Is Speaking:
Are You Listening?

Are you ready to make and keep your new life's career resolutions just by listening when God speaks and doing what you hear him say? You can do this by finding the biblical scriptures that can help you meet your goals.

This book was designed with students and young people in mind, but adults will enjoy this book also.

The "Someone is Speaking Moment" is where God talks to you through his word.

The "Are You Listening Moment" is the time for you to truly reflect on what God said and see how it applies to your life.

This book aims to help you understand God's Word and see how it applies to your life today.

ISBN 978-0-9832682-1-5 $12.00 U.S.
$17.00 Can.

www.ingramcontent.com/pod-product-compliance
Lightning Source LLC
Chambersburg PA
CBHW071102090426

42737CB00013B/2440